ALL THE HILLS

All the Hills

poems by

Brian Glaser

Shanti Arts Publishing
Brunswick, Maine

ALL THE HILLS

Copyright © 2019 Brian Glaser

All rights reserved. No part of this book may be used or reproduced in any manner whatsoever without the written permission of the publisher.

Published by Shanti Arts Publishing

Cover and interior design
by Shanti Arts Designs

Image on cover by
Rucksack Magazine / unsplash.com

Shanti Arts LLC
Brunswick, Maine
www.shantiarts.com

Printed in the United States of America

ISBN: 978-1-947067-96-7

LCCN: 2019948426

for Melanie

Contents

Pueblo Sin Fronteras	11
Bradstreet Prayer-Sail	12
Talking to Casas	14
Over All the Hills	15
To John, for His Tenth Birthday	28
Four Cantos on Enlightenment	33
As Winter	39
The Snow Angel	41
The Dark Ages	45

Saltwater Wetlands

Mallard Duck	51
American Coots	52
Coastal Sunset	53
Pigeon	54
Snowy Egret	55
Saltgrass	56
Bottle	57
Snowy Plover	58
Snowy Plover	59
Mount Saddleback	60
The Seagull	61
Brown Pelican	62
Estuary Prospect	63
Mudflats	64

About the Author	67

Acknowledgments

Grateful acknowledgment is made to the editors of the following publications where these poems first appeared:

Poets Reading the News: "Pueblo Sin Fronteras"

Little Rose Magazine: "Bradstreet Prayer-Sail"

Amethyst Review: Cantos 1 and 3 of "Four Cantos on Enlightenment"

Oddball Magazine: "As Winter"

Otoliths: "The Dark Ages"

Pueblo Sin Fronteras

For many years as a man
I did not care
where I was to be buried.

And then I visited
a distant cemetery
for months, for years.

Where I would like to be buried
there is an iron wall
and a gate
that is locked in the evening.

Fear is the great wall
against music,

so we must flee it together,
we who want to live,
and those who travel by night —

which is to say all of us,
sadly,
prayerfully.

Bradstreet Prayer-Sail

1.
Shad in the ground,
doubles.

Grace in the heat
of the weather.

Who says profit
and righteousness
was not one thing

in the unborn world?

No,
stay with me
on the grassy shore
of ever.

2.
Retrospect,
the photo of the guide.

Compost,
the Bibliothek.

You give me courage
to write to my children

about the sun.

About the wind,
what it did to my bed.

3.
Goodness is not a matter of rules.
It is an emanation.
It grows cold.

The stolen book
redeems the whole encampment.

The mayor
of the encampment
wakes

the hounds,

wakes the tear.

4.
If you love it,
call it dark.

The blind bird
becomes the college
when he doubts —

all the salt in the oceans
and still this
freshwater rivulet.

Talking to Casas

Melancholy priest,
the red leaf of spring.

Over All the Hills

1.
And so summer begins, on a June evening,
and I wonder whether we will make it
to Tuolumne Meadows in Yosemite this year
as we always wish to do, as we often have
since our lives in California began again
thirteen summers ago.
Those meadows are favored by a river
memorable to whoever has seen it —
to see it is to step into it up over the ankle.
What makes those meadows survive,
with their low grasses and pines at the margins,
is the mountain snowmelt which leaves the soil
so soft that no tree can take root.
Miwok is the name the people gave themselves
who were living here before
the European settlers came.
Matthias Glaser, born in Germany,
father of William, who fathered Clarence,
who fathered John, who fathered me —
what could Matthias have seen
of the war-hatched Europe he fled that would compare
with the gentle, eviscerating beauty
of these meadows?

2.
To conserve the meadows in the park
as public land, open to all who pay the fee,
the Miwok were displaced;
extirpated might be the most apt word.
Some encroachers, like Muir and Roosevelt,
were outright white supremacists,
while others seem to have thought of themselves
as enlightened realists, doing the best thing
for everybody by evicting
indigenous people from their land,
a process that was wholly realized
not until the nineteen sixties.
At a protest last week against the separation
of parents and children who arrive at the US border
seeking asylum, my son, John,
moved down the city hall steps a little distance from me,
into the crowd of about a hundred,
and then he left the crowd on the steps
and walked down the sloping lawn
and behind the cameras
before he circled around to me again on the top step
and asked to sit on my shoulders.
And so for the best part of an hour I stood
with him claiming me,
holding above his head a sign I made the day before
which read, in plain black print:
ABOLISH ICE.

3.
There is beauty in our efforts to be good,
though it's perilously easy
to be ignorant or dumb about their confluence —
a book on the subject written at the end
of the last century
makes much of how beauty renders perceptible
the fair,
and the philosopher who wrote it misses all or most
of the essential irony of that word
in that context, the way
that it means light-skinned and blond haired
as well as just.
The system is fair,
a disgusted colleague from Japan said of our college,
and her contempt for the innocent use of the word
impressed me as something
I would never again wish to be on the wrong side of.

Moral beauty
is about more than the superego's gestures
because beauty always has
a dimension of the private —
the invitation to it, the longing for it.

4.
There was a riot in Cincinnati —
the birthplace of William and Clarence and John —
in the year 1884.
Gilded Age Cincinnati
was rife with corruption, and many young men
wanted to lynch
a young black man who had killed a white man
and had not been sentenced to death.
The riot lasted for days,
the Ohio National Guard was called upon,
and many were killed in a conflict that one historian
has described as irrational.
The Paris Commune had raised the stakes for everyone.
There were socialists and communists and anarchists,
by the hundreds,
and perhaps a number of Catholics too.
That was the path my branch of the Glasers took —
adherence to the band of the faithful, the religious,
the law from Rome sent to Cincinnati.

5.
If beauty involves dissolution
of the boundary between the public and the private,
a field of mutual presence,
perhaps many find the subject of beauty jejune
because celebrating the private
forms a crucial part of the neoliberal syndrome
that afflicts the globe,
rewarding avarice, even in the abstract,
and teaching us a bottomless lesson of cynicism,
to fear each other and objectify ourselves.

I see and understand this point of view:
the private is too much with us;
the public is the political.
Yet what door does not have two sides—?

6.
And so for the past week I have been living
in a timeshare resort in Palm Desert
with a patio that leads to a path that leads
down to a canal
where there are ducks and geese and turtles
that fascinate my daughter.
She walks out to them first thing in the morning
and takes pictures of them with her phone.
On the slope on the other side of the canal
there was a man working today in long sleeves and pants
in 115-degree heat.
We marveled at his endurance over lunch.
Maybe, my son suggested,
he has children that he needs to support
and he has to work this job.

This is the story of the summer —
the heat, the leisure, the familiar presences
of my children to me, and me to them;
the sense that this is more like eternity than the other seasons,
that there is a secret to it
that I will learn if I am patient,
patient and good.

7.
The Attorney General
has cited scripture in defense of the separation
of refugee children from their parents.
And my cousin and many others have responded
by citing the chapter in Matthew's gospel
where Jesus says
what you do for the least of my brothers
you do for me.
It was my father's favorite passage of the Bible,
perhaps of any piece of writing.
We are surrounded, my small family of four,
by those who pray —
grandmothers, aunts and uncles, cousins.
My mother told me that she baptized my children
while giving them baths.
Sometimes my decision to go without the church
feels like choosing the bracing air
of a mountain meadow
as a constant companion.

8.
Xylem sap is one of two kinds found in living trees.
It moves from the roots to the leaves
carrying nutrients and minerals.
There are still competing theories about how
the sap rises, contravening gravity.
Its potential to rise acts
as a limit on the growth, the height of trees like the maple —
a tree that grew in the yard of my third home,
whose leaves are redder than blood in autumn
and from which we made maple syrup in the spring.

Yesterday I left my son at camp for a week
in the San Jacinto mountains.
It is on a ridge surrounded by slopes of pines.
When we went to Joshua Tree during our desert vacation
I marveled aloud to my children
at the traceries of deep cracks between the rocks,
the way the sandy surface and black lines
indicate the presence of two opposing inclinations of matter —
to cohere and to fissure,
to be one and to be many,
or to be something and nothing at once.
Driving from the desert to the mountains,
I found myself on the side of
the green that appears as you ascend,
the inhabitant, the survivor-surface that says yes —
but yes to what?

9.
What are you about?
Allen Ginsberg asks in a poem.

On Father's Day, yesterday,
some talked about what their fathers had taught them.

My son on my shoulders, at the top of a stair,
holding above his head a placard.

Think about what that sign should say:
so my father taught me.

10.
The caretaker at my wife's sister's beach house
in the city of El Garitón, Guatemala
asked me
years after we had met,
with a kind of modest fascination,
if children on the American side of the border,
por ahí,
are born speaking English
or whether we learn to speak from our parents, too,
like the infant ladinos of the coast.

11.
Perhaps they are right,
those whom I have pitied a little for their coldness,
perhaps the concept of fatherhood is eutrophic.
This sudden ferocity in America to imagine
with an exclusive claim to virtue
how we should welcome the children arriving at our southern border.
It's a crisis because
the family is how we as a nation care for young people
and so this concept makes its way
into the reserve of who we think we are
as a society,
where we do and do not want it to be.

12.
Colleagues at work, liberal friends, my apolitical mother—
everyone has within two days been panic stricken
about the separation of families,
and when we protested two weeks ago in downtown LA
there were a hundred of us
out of millions around.
Now Trump has reversed himself and my daughter is rightly proud
that we won, as she says,
that we helped to lead the way.
The Pope has weighed in today:
"A person's dignity does not depend on them being a citizen,
a migrant, or a refugee.
Saving the life of someone fleeing war and poverty
is an act of humanity."

And Obama offers some bullshit
about shared values and ideals,
and yet being big enough to uphold our laws.
Whitman wrote a racist poem,
"O Pioneers!"
There are over a million bacterial organisms
living in my body—
they create my scat but they are not me.

13.
Today:

I was sitting against the wall in the courtyard,
my wife was gardening,
my daughter was in the pool.

The overhanging roof
shaded me from the sun.

I closed my eyes and leaned my head back.
A slight breeze moved across the pool
and reached me.

A voice spoke to me.
You are deeply, deeply loved,
it said.

And I felt that it was true.
What is this, I thought.

Is it okay, I asked the voice,
if I call you poetry?

Yes, said the voice.

14.
A year ago I searched the poems
of Marianne Moore for a veiled statement of ethical regret
about teaching
at the Carlisle Indian School.

I may have found one. I'm not sure yet.

But what precisely were the crimes, I ask a year later,
in which she was implicated,
she who taught there unhappily for years?

Forcible removal of children from their families.
Racist exclusion of their own cultures from the curriculum.

And: what else?

Which word is endangered, yes or no?
Yes is superfluous.
No is like irony.

Hope is a way of relating to the present.
Hope is a question.

To John, for His Tenth Birthday

Act One

1.
A day at the beach for you
Is self-evident sun.

I am through dwelling on the right of return
This Sunday afternoon

While you listen to music
Under a blanket by the shore.

Learn from me:
I learned from you.

2.
It is uncertain
On which day erotic love

Will unbind the universe
I think of as your room;

All your books will remain there at first,
The vertical, the horizontal —

Among them a story
Unfinished forever.

3.
The name of the father —
There must be some other law

That binds us,
As when Kenny Aronson's father

Stood and spoke to him
Before us all at his bar mitzvah.

We know we change
By being loved as who we were.

Act Two

4.
Dad, you seem depressed,
you said to me yesterday.

As if to say: how could I be depressed
with a son like you?

And yet, of course,
I cannot keep us from our mortal fate,

Though I can hide my sadness
Under all the hills.

5.
Everyone has a secret,
a student said in class.

Man sholde nat knowe
Of Goddes pryvetee —

In a lost religion
Reposes the god of time —

Everyone has a kind of happiness
In God's privacy —

6.
The point of narrative
Is life after death:

That's why you like it.
It keeps the narrator alive.

Act Three

7.
The text of science will be true
A million years from now.

The scriptures have
To be invented

And so they can't be true.
So science is the sacred book

And where it is silent
Is its keenest test.

8.
The error is to think of science
As the brainchild of the West —

And it is a short step from there
To the brainchild of the Jews.

But you, with your first word,
Confirmed that the globe

Is like the ball you named —
Discovered each day anew.

9.
On our evening walk tonight you excoriated
Those who believe the earth is flat.

Most historians are conventional people,
As are most therapists — thank God.

Are scientists in headlong escape
From the questions keeping me awake?

And what are those questions —
Guards against the portals of my dream?

Four Cantos on Enlightenment

1.
The fire had worked its local menace,
The waiter and the boat rental manager
Had stories about how close the disaster

Had come this time, about the heroism of the fighters
And the ordinary evil of the arsonist
Who was out on bond for burning a barn.

We were camping not far from Lake Hemet.
The manager brought us to a corner
With a map of the lake and showed us where

We might find two bald eagles alighting
Or launching out from a wood along the lakeside.
They raise their young here, he said,

Because food is plentiful in the lake,
But there is not enough for more than two adults
And so, when it is time, you can find them

Chasing off their offspring over the water,
Insisting with wing and talon that their parenting
Work is over. So are they strangers, then?

I was not adept at motoring the boat
Out of the inlet through a shallow throat
Of water and into the manmade lake.

It took a few tries. I think sometimes of
My great grandfathers — but less often
Of my great grandmothers and the women

In my family tree from an age yet older than theirs.
Did they ever imagine me, the Irish Catholic
Orphan from New Jersey and the German-born

Mother of eight in a Cincinnati ghetto?
Did they have hopes that I would be —
A doctor? A bishop? The mayor of a nearby town?

A father, perhaps? Well, I am a decent person
And in every respect a grown man.
I find it hard to think of myself chasing anyone off

The way those eagles have to do.
But I want no part anymore of
The religion they promulgated, my great grandmothers,

Zealously or dutifully or both.
I am afraid that even citizenship among the saved
Mostly feels to me like a flare thrown

On a forest road, from a car in which,
According to eyewitness reports,
There is either one person, or there are two.

2.
I don't remember where I heard of Nietzsche
But I recall knowing that he was valuable
As I read him lying on the grassy bank

Of Strawberry Creek in Berkeley
During my first week of classes there.
Cliché upon cliché — but I was the only one

There with him on that afternoon.
Hannah Arendt hated the hackneyed
Language of Adolph Eichmann,

And one biographer says that's because
According to her politics everyone should be
Expected to express themselves in an original way.

Science is to the Enlightenment as the flood that
Straightens out the meandering track the river
Had cut itself along. What good are the arts to our species,

Evolved as we are by chance from the apes?
I asked my students. One woman — brilliant,
Who wrote about the war on femininity

And gave me and my family a discount at the pizzeria
On the circle in town — answered in a tone of
Uncertain conviction: They help keep us sane.

3.
My first word as a child was light.
My mother brought me into dark rooms
And spoke the word as she flipped the switch

And one day at around twelve months
I said the word before she did.
I had a concept and its sound: marked by history.

And months before that I had been taken
Away from her and put through
A spinal tap as a neonate

Because I had spinal meningitis.
Twenty hours separated as a newborn
And subjected to excruciating pain alone.

So when I talk to you, when I pose a question
To you, I have come to understand why
I do not wholly expect that you will answer.

After the First World War it became
Thinkable to hate the Enlightenment,
As Horkheimer and Adorno did.

What do I have left if I join them —
If I try to return to the dark room
And instead of choosing the concept —

Discovering it again as we may perpetually do —
I sit in silence, rejecting the shared word,
The half-credible evidence of a bond restored?

4.
Sartre says that we are condemned to be free:
Sometimes, knowing that there is no creator,
We do not wish it to be so.

A blogger says that Sartre is useful
In adolescence and at midlife.
My high school girlfriend,

Whom I did not love,
Was late for her menstruation after
I had tried to use two condoms at once inexpertly

And they both came off.
I don't know what I would have done.
Around this time my English teacher

Was lecturing to us about Sartre
And the absurdity of the world.
Once we have chosen not to commit suicide,

He said, we are at every moment
Responsible and free.
For a long time I thought studying obsessively

One writer was like being a fascist.
I have come to see that it is more like being a parent.
We feel it is urgent to know well

The psyche, the soul, of the person we love,
And we don't wish to judge them,
We wish to help them create

Themselves most fully as others know them.
Your grandfather was special,
The CEO of my father's hospital corporation

Told my daughter at a reception
On the grounds of the Sisters a few years
After my father had died.

Everyone is special, my daughter said.
Everyone is unique, the executive said.
But your grandfather was special.

As Winter

— 26 November, 2018

1.
Why winter?
Season of the cyclamen,

the burn
the fire walks on.

From dark to dark
the sun
shines through a glass.

Will winter ever
uncover or weather

a rattle's depth
at the early end of its dream?

The trader-trophy,
the snow —

2.
People are talking about you,
ukulele.

It is quiet though
in the Christmas tree fields.

The answer forks
into another answer,

and so on,
like a dancer's walking.

They are playing a game.
A time, a shame.

A crime,
a game with their spray,

a litter of letters,
a sky of clouds

after the right moon might
go away.

The Snow Angel

1.
My teacher,
who showed us all afternoon how to hollow out
the heart of a mountain of snow—
he slept there with us,
the six of us or so,
schoolchildren on a winter Michigan excursion
as far as we could bear from home,
trusting the ton of mounded snow above us to be clement
as we slept in its den.

Now I cannot remember his name,
or the names of any of us,
the chosen ones
who slept outdoors one night at nature camp—

so I will call him
the first angel.

2.
The second angel
came to take my father when I was thirteen years old.

She let him stay with us
and moved us all to California.

On her recruiting visit one winter evening,
she,
a gray-haired nun,
Corrine,
marveled at the falling snow,
at and after sundown,
whitening the view out through the window
of our front yard.

She said she had never seen snow falling before.

She loved my father,
and though I didn't want her to move us
I think I marveled at her gratefully for that —

for showing me that,
as he came home after dark,
my father had left somewhere else
where he had made something that made him loved.

3.
And there is the snow falling
at the end of the stunningly beautiful story
by Joyce,
the snow that falls on the living and the dead.

And it is a discovery —
how much one shares with the dead,
a discovery particular to
the long summer twilight of adolescence
in which one comes, first and best,
to that story.

The third angel is me,
pushing a Bronco out of a rut of snow
in the mountains one winter
in Running Springs.

There were others there, too,
none of whom I am close to now,
all of us a little stunned to be so young and feel so free,
if memory is true across these many years,
all of us discovering our power
in each other,

in every way just like the mutinous snow.

4.
My daughter's first winter
was in Duesseldorf,
where we had a few friends.

One of them was a compatriot of Melanie's,
another Guatemalan living there,
engaged to a lawyer
who lived a ten-minute walk from our flat.

One evening after our dinner she slept in her pram
as we walked home

and the snow was falling on us and around us,
a family of three,
no one on the street ahead of us

and we were unable to see to the end of the street
because of the depth of the snow

and I felt a rare, blessed feeling to me
when living abroad,
that my experience suddenly symbolized something,
meant something else, to someone else,

though I can not to this day
say what that symbolism is,

though my heart leaps up, sometimes, a little, still,
when our gate closes noisily behind my wife
as she comes home.

The Dark Ages

1.
Europe thinking.
Silent nights

where they would ask
one another

what day had seen.

Learning is
the gentlest faith:

O my god —
make of my mistakes

the light
you denied

without knowing.

2.
The barn
will grow more dense

there,
the prophets

speak backwards,

the trace
will be ordinary

as the crisp pronunciation
of a child.

3.
My pride
at healing and being healed

is not quite

a thousand years old,

young
for an art.

It waited for me

to listen
to myself.

4.
And the silence deepens,

a salary
as a gift —

it was the error
of the beaten path.

5.
My enemy
loved me like a friend.

I was blessed
with four.

An innocent mistake —

that is why
they hated me,

my love
descended

from the darker age.

Saltwater Wetlands

Mallard Duck

We were hunted here generations ago;
it was a matter of principle

and dark pleasure to exterminate us one by one.

You've lived in the long aftermath,
you know why

you looked in vain for us at the reserve today.

They call us an invasive species.

Perhaps they are right—
I should not speak for all of us

but I have not yet lost faith
that we too may find our place among the races on this earth.

American Coots

We amused you today,
paddling in wide loops in the tidal estuary,
me and my five hatchlings.

So urgently purposive we seemed to be,
moving in a strict, arcing line in the water

until one of the little ones
broke the spell of seriousness

by following another direction impetuously
and we became again a chaotic family,

unsure of the force of the rules binding us together,
like any other.

I think the same thing brought both of us to this wetland —
an idea of peace,
a place to help us keep our commitments.

But what happened to you
when all five hatchlings disappeared under water

one at a time,
each following another by some instinct
neither of us understands,

and you watched me, the lone parent among the wild birds here,
solitary gray on the vast gray of the water
for what seemed a full minute —

that wasn't peace you felt —
that was freedom.

Coastal Sunset

You want to leave already.
Strange, the stories of those who find my sadness

too much to bear.
That is not why you want to leave.

Nor are you afraid of what I will
remind you of.

You believe in progress — it is simple as that.
We disagree.

I will make you an offer:
You stay until I am ready to release you

and I will give you a haunting image of my sister,
the estuary at dawn.

Pigeon

I like human beings —
you understand what I'm trying to say.

I like how
the miracle of human consciousness
so often seems ordinary to them,

how they walk past each other
as if there were nothing remarkable in them at all.

That deep, creaturely cooing that I make
perched on a beam under the walkway
as they pass —

I know it reminds them somewhat eerily
of the universals of human experience,

music and mothering —

it is uncanny because it is supposed to be,
my heartening critique.

Snowy Egret

You think the image you captured
of me alone in the eelgrass

means something because when you came close
on the walkway bridge
I didn't leave you standing there bereft?

You believe what generations of boyish men
have believed about faithfulness.

Look,
look at all this —
the only word for it is beautiful,

the living surface of the planes of water
and the sheer joy
in its blinding lovemaking with the sun,

everything you missed studying me
as I stood watching prey in the water unmoving,
a vessel for your art.

And now you want me to show it to you,
now that we both have left
this corner of paradise —

experience is a far better teacher for you now —
she has some faith left in you.

Saltgrass

I live on
what kills others like me.

The wetlands that have been destroyed
by civilization,

and the remade, the intact —
they are all my natural beds.

The secret to surviving the inrush
of salt from the ocean

is to let it pass right through you —
it is like solving a difficult riddle:

the mistake of so many
is to see in it a part of themselves.

Bottle

You trouble yourself
with your incessant doubts about the afterlife.

I represent your deeper fear,
the one your dread of nothingness
is a screen against.

I will outlive this estuary,
eroding slowly over centuries, floating wherever
the currents take me.

I have been loved by nothing but myself.

I hate the world that made me:
I wish with a burning resentment against my fate
that I had never been.

Snowy Plover

We have been warned
to consider the dangers of fake wisdom —

hated by poets
I suppose because it is a guardian of ignorance,

the inverse of the sanctuaries
protected for us on the southern coast of California,

where the poets can go months without seeing any of us
and can bear uncertainty —

They call it negative capability:
imagination as a habitat,

a coastal garden
where the living heart rests in its quest to survive.

Snowy Plover

And because there are many of us
we cannot speak with one voice.

It is like their theory of money—
that because the desire for it can explain human behavior

there must be no other motives involved.

They are the sentimental ones, you know.
The dunes of Bolsa Chica

change with imperceptible slowness
not because they are made of sand
but because the wind here

disappears and reappears from elsewhere,
a calling to each of us.

Mount Saddleback

You like moments
when deep feeling carefully finds expression,

the traces in its play
of subtlety and nuance,
buds in the black branches you seek out and remember.

So you covet the authority of the observer:

let me remind you, friend,
that your father is one among the shades
you love so intensely —

you have not yet said to the world anything
he can be well remembered by.

The creative imagination is simply
an alibi for you.

The difference between a society and its culture
is like the difference between

an ordinary father and his brilliant child —

so say I, a mountain that has seen three empires,
waiting, patiently, for you to ascend —

patiently, as you read on.

The Seagull

Are you ready for absence yet?—
so asked the seagull.

Her white wings were spread wide open
to receive the air,

her body shadowless
on an overcast afternoon.

So a lover opened herself to me, once,
wordlessly—
her legs stretched out beneath my thrusting form,

as if straining to receive me whole,
to welcome me.

Art can haunt,
and flight is an art—

its meaning to mortals is clear and incontrovertible
when it is framed by our desire.

Brown Pelican

I marvel at you humans
who mate for life.

Do you feel you must?

Perhaps if you could fly things would be different.

I am not a beautiful bird,
I do not promise anyone happiness —

I make predictions —

that art is how
I know when to rip up the tranquil surface and find life.

Estuary Prospect

Benches: four of them,
a semi-circular pattern, no more than a quarter mile into the reserve
from the north gate parking lot —

you can hear very well from there
the cars racing by on the Korean war veterans' highway,
the way we all come and go.

From above the benches must look
like the arms of a vast lyre of dirt.

From there you can hear
the mullet leap through the sub-tidal water's surface —

some say their dreams only whisper in shards,
some say every poem is an artifice,
the end —

I have long known that poets first think of their last poem on waking,

but now I see that there is only
the one poem,

the unfinished hymn that sings them through.

Mudflats

My great sadness is
that the life I know returns like the clouds.

At ebb-tide
they have a touching patience with me—
my softness, my secrets.

Yet I am made
to be visible to them only in ordinary time—
they keep for the marsh-ground

their bodily trust,
their deepest passion,
the bonded pairs.

My secret is
how cautiously all species evolve—

the single tern from the marshes
means more to me
than he does to nature,

but I cannot tell him so—

my silence is a language
forgotten like friendship at the end of life.

About the Author

Brian Glaser was born in Detroit, Michigan, the eldest of two children of Jack Glaser, a theologian, and Mary Ellen Glaser, an educator and social worker. He was educated at the University of California, Berkeley. In 2003, he married dancer and choreographer Melanie Ríos, with whom he has two children, Andoe and John. In 2005, he joined the faculty at Chapman University, where he currently teaches in the department of English.

SHANTI ARTS
NATURE · ART · SPIRIT

Please visit us on online

to browse our entire book catalog,

including additional poetry collections and fiction,

books on travel, nature, healing, art,

photography, and more.

shantiarts.com

www.ingramcontent.com/pod-product-compliance
Lightning Source LLC
Chambersburg PA
CBHW070451050426
42451CB00015B/3439